GETTING TO KNOW THE WORLD'S GREATEST ARTISTS

JOHANNES
VERMEER

WRITTEN AND ILLUSTRATED BY MIKE VENEZIA

CHILDREN'S PRESS®
A DIVISION OF SCHOLASTIC INC.
NEW YORK   TORONTO   LONDON   AUCKLAND   SYDNEY
MEXICO CITY   NEW DELHI   HONG KONG
DANBURY, CONNECTICUT

To Carol Ritzmann Leonard, with whom I enjoyed many
spirited discussions about Vermeer.

Cover: *The Milkmaid,* by Johannes Vermeer. c. 1660, oil on canvas, 45.5 x 41 cm.
© Rijksmuseum Amsterdam.

Colorist for illustrations: Liz Venezia

Library of Congress Cataloging-in-Publication Data

Venezia, Mike.
     Johannes Vermeer / written and illustrated by Mike Venezia.
         p. c.m. — (Getting to know the world's greatest artists)
     Summary: An overview of the life and work of the seventeenth-century Dutch painter, famous for
creating realistic scenes of everyday life.
       ISBN 0-516-22282-1 (lib. bdg.)   0-516-26999-2 (pbk.)
       1. Vermeer, Johannes, 1632-1675—Juvenile literature. 2. Painters—Netherlands—Biography—
Juvenile literature. [1. Vermeer, Johannes, 1632-1675. 2. Artists. 3. Painting, Dutch. 4. Art appreciation.]
I. Vermeer, Johannes, 1632-1675. II. Title.

ND653.V5 V38 2002
759.9492—dc21
[B]
                                                                                    2001047194

Copyright 2002 by Mike Venezia.
All rights reserved. Published simultaneously in Canada
Printed in China.
16 17 18 19 20 R 20 19 18   62

Scholastic Inc., 557 Broadway, New York, NY 10012.

Johannes Vermeer was born in Delft, Holland, in 1632. Hardly anything is known about his life. He never even made a portrait of himself. The famous Vermeer painting above shows an artist in his studio. The artist might be Johannes, but no one knows for sure.

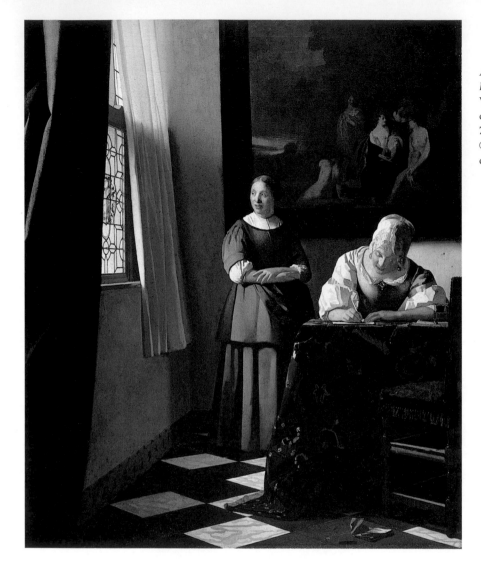

Even though the story of Johannes Vermeer's life is a mystery, his paintings are known and loved by people all over the world. Vermeer chose familiar, everyday subjects. His paintings usually show one or two people in a room, with light coming in through a window.

Young Woman with a Water Jug, by Johannes Vermeer. c. 1664, oil on canvas, 45.7 x 40.6 cm.
© Metropolitan Museum of Art, Marquand Collection, Gift of Henry G. Marquand, 1889, (89.15.21).

What makes these paintings so wonderful is the awesome quiet and stillness Vermeer was able to create.

When you look at a Vermeer painting, it feels almost like you're sharing a real moment with someone who lived in Holland more than 300 years ago.

Woman in Blue Reading Letter, by Johannes Vermeer. c. 1662, oil on canvas, 46.5 x 39 cm.
© Rijksmuseum Amsterdam.

A View of Delft, with Musical Instrument Seller's Stall, by Carel Fabritius. 1652, oil on canvas, 15.5 x 31.7 cm. © National Gallery, London.

In 1632, when Johannes Vermeer was born, Holland was becoming one of the wealthiest and most powerful countries in Europe. The Dutch had just won an 80-year-long war against their Spanish rulers. People in Holland couldn't wait to show the world how proud they were of their new freedom.

The Dutch began to explore undiscovered parts of the world and set up colonies there. They made lots of money trading cloth and other goods, including a type of pottery called Delft porcelain. These beautiful dishes, bowls, and vases—which are still popular today—

were made right in Vermeer's own city. The Dutch were also known at the time for their discoveries in science, medicine, and astronomy.

Delft ware vase with floral decoration. 1670-1721. © Art Resource, NY/Réunion des Musées Nationaux, Musée National de Ceramique, Sevres, France, photo by M. Beck-Coppola.

Holland was also an exciting center for art during this time. Some of the greatest artists of all time lived and worked in Holland in the 1600s.

Family Group, by Rembrandt van Rijn. c. 1667, oil on canvas, 126 x 167 cm. © Herzog Anton Ulrich-Museums, Braunschweig, photo by B.P. Keiser.

Marriage Portrait of Isaac Massa and Beatrix van der Laen, by Frans Hals. 1622, oil on canvas, 140 x 166.5 cm. © Rijksmuseum Amsterdam.

The Apple Peeler, by Gerard Ter Borch. c. 1661, oil on wood, 36.3 x 30.7 cm. © Kunsthistorisches Museum, Vienna.

The Feast of Saint Nicholas, by Jan Steen. c. 1663, oil on canvas, 82 x 70 cm. © Rijksmuseum Amsterdam.

Interior with Women beside a Linen Chest, by Pieter de Hooch. 1663, oil on canvas, 68 x 59 cm. © Rijksmuseum Amsterdam.

Frans Hals, Rembrandt van Rijn, Pieter de Hooch, Jan Steen, Gerard Ter Borch, and many others created so many beautiful paintings in Holland that this time in European history became known as the Golden Age of Art!

As the Old Sing, So Twitter the Young, by Jan Steen. 1663, oil on canvas, 134 x 163 cm.
© Art Resource, NY/Mauritshuis, The Hague, Netherlands.

While Johannes Vermeer was growing up, his father was very busy. Mr. Vermeer owned and ran an inn like the one shown in the painting above. He also sold silk cloth and was an art dealer. It wasn't unusual back then for hotels and inns to display and sell artwork.

There isn't a word written about Johannes Vermeer's childhood, but he must have seen lots of paintings from all over the world when he was a kid. He must also have learned to draw and paint from one of the many excellent artists in his city.

Mary with Child and Saints Catharina, Cecilia, Barbara and Ursula, by Master of the Virgo inter Virgines, oil on panel, 123 x 102 cm. © Rijksmuseum Amsterdam.

During the Golden Age of Art, artists worked differently than they had in the past. When the Spanish king ruled, Dutch artists were hired to make artwork for the walls of royal palaces and churches.

The Surrender of Breda, by Diego Velazquez. Before 1635, oil on canvas, 307 x 367 cm. © Museo Nacional del Prado, Madrid.

The only acceptable things to paint were portraits of wealthy royal people, and scenes of historical battles, legends, or stories from the Bible.

The Fish Seller, by Adriaen van Ostade. 1673, oil on canvas, 36.5 x 39.5 cm. © Rijksmuseum Amsterdam.

The Goldfinch, by Carel Fabritius. 1654, oil on panel, 33.5 x 22.8. © Art Resource, NY/Scala/Mauritshuis, The Hague, Netherlands.

Without kings and religious leaders telling artists what to paint, Dutch artists began to make paintings of whatever they and their customers liked. Most people in Holland had enough money now to afford paintings for their homes. The most popular pictures were scenes from everyday life.

These pictures were called genre paintings. Soon it seemed as if everyone in Holland had these types of paintings hanging in their homes and workplaces.

Christ in the House of Martha and Mary, by Johannes Vermeer. c. 1655, oil on canvas, 160 x 142 cm. © National Gallery of Scotland, Edinburgh, Dean Gallery, photo by Antonia Reeve.

When Johannes Vermeer started out, he did his paintings in the older style, using ideas from Bible stories and mythology. Before long, though, he shifted to doing scenes from everyday life.

A Maid Asleep is one of Vermeer's first genre paintings. It includes some of the things Johannes would put in his paintings throughout his life, such as a decorative tablecloth

Diana and Her Companions, by Johannes Vermeer. c. 1655, oil on canvas, 98 x 105 cm. © Art Resource, NY/Scala/Mauritshuis, The Hague, Netherlands.

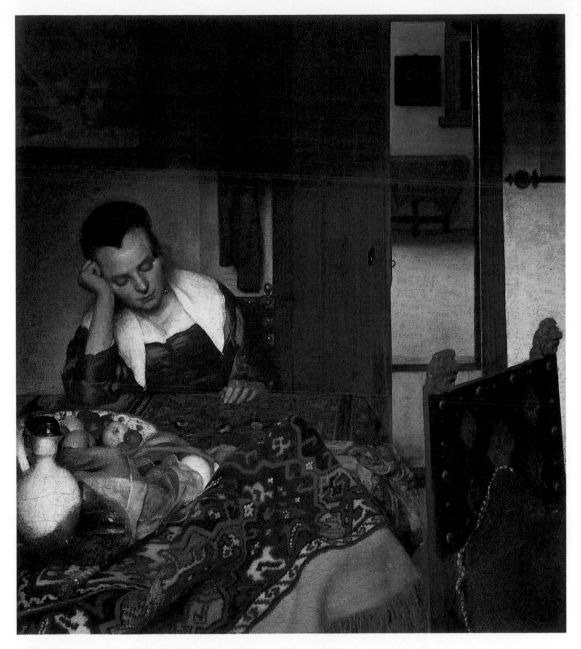

A Maid Asleep, by Johannes Vermeer. 1657, oil on canvas, 87.6 x 76.5 cm.
© Metropolitan Museum of Art, Bequest of Benjamin Altman, 1913, (14.40.611).

with an interesting still life on top of it. The painting also has that special feeling of quiet stillness found in many of Vermeer's paintings.

In 1652, when Johannes Vermeer was
20 years old, his father died. Johannes took
over his father's art business and ran the inn.
He became even busier when he married
Catharina Bolnes a year later.

Johannes and Catharina ended up having fifteen children! Johannes Vermeer made only about forty paintings during his whole life. It's amazing he had enough time to do any paintings at all.

The Geographer, by Johannes Vermeer. 1669, oil on canvas, 53 x 46.6 cm.
© Städelsches Kunstinstitut, Frankfurt/Artothek/Blauel-Gnamm.

Even though Johannes Vermeer became one of Delft's most popular artists, he couldn't make a living just by painting pictures. Hardly any artist could at that time.

Suddenly there were so many artists
around that paintings were being sold all over
for very little money. Some artists even sold
their works from booths in the marketplace.

Street in Delft, by Johannes Vermeer.
c. 1657, oil on canvas, 54.3 x 44 cm.
© Rijksmuseum Amsterdam.

Most of Johannes Vermeer's paintings are of people. He did paint two beautiful city scenes, though. One is called *Street in Delft.* The other, *View of Delft,* is one of Vermeer's greatest works. You can feel Johannes Vermeer's love for his city. The unusual lighting gives the feeling of a moody day just after a storm has passed through. The houses and buildings seem to sparkle as the sun shines down on them from behind a cloud.

View of Delft, Netherlands, After the Fire, by Johannes Vermeer. c. 1658, oil on canvas, 98.5 x 117.5 cm.
© Art Resource, NY/Mauritshuis, The Hague, Netherlands, photo by Erich Lessing.

In this special painting, Johannes Vermeer lets you know exactly what it was like to be standing outside his city in the late 1660s.

The sparkly feeling Vermeer created in *View of Delft* also shows up in some of his other paintings. The little glowing and reflective dots and globs he used reminds many people of light reflections that can be seen in photographs.

In *Girl with the Red Hat,* you can see sparkly dots on the girl's nose, lips, earring, and polished chair decoration. Cameras weren't invented until almost 200 years later. But people in Holland, including Vermeer, were very interested in seeing how things looked through a glass lens. The best telescopes and microscopes in Europe were being made in Holland during the 1600s.

Girl with the Red Hat, by Johannes Vermeer. c. 1665, oil on panel, 22.8 x 18 cm. © National Gallery of Art, Washington, D.C., Andrew W. Mellon Collection, photo by Richard Carafelli.

In one of Vermeer's most famous paintings, *The Lace Maker,* the objects in front of the girl are a little bit out of focus. This is how a camera lens can make things look. Johannes knew this would cause your eye to focus right away on the busy girl. The little lacemaker is concentrating so hard on what she's doing that it's easy to feel like you're working right along with her.

The Lace Maker, by Johannes Vermeer. c. 1669, oil on canvas, 24 x 21 cm.
©Art Resource, NY/Réunion des Musées Nationaux, Louvre, Paris, France.

The Milkmaid,
by Johannes Vermeer.
c. 1660, oil on canvas,
45.5 x 41 cm.
©Rijksmuseum
Amsterdam.

It's fun to look for the realistic details
Johannes Vermeer included in his paintings.
Sometimes you'll notice a nail hole in the wall
or the reflection of a person in the window.

Vermeer worked very carefully to capture his people in a moment of deep thought. His beautiful lighting, use of perspective, and simple compositions make his paintings as close to perfect as possible.

Johannes Vermeer died in 1675 at the age o. 43. For almost 200 years, he was forgotten. His paintings were scattered all over Europe and were often mistaken for the work of other artists, such as Rembrandt or Pieter de Hooch. Finally, in the late 1800s, people began to realize that these amazing paintings were the work of one great artist—Johannes Vermeer.

The works of art in this book came from:

The Frick Collection, New York
Herzog Anton Ulrich-Museums, Braunschweig
Kunsthistorisches Museum, Vienna
Louvre, Paris
Mauritshuis, The Hague
Metropolitan Museum of Art, New York
Museo Nacional del Prado, Madrid
National Gallery, London
National Gallery of Art, Washington, D.C.
National Gallery of Ireland, Dublin
National Gallery of Scotland, Edinburgh
Rijksmuseum, Amsterdam
Staatliche Kunstsammlungen, Dresden
Städelsches Kunstinstitut, Frankfurt